Lumen Christi...
Holy Wisdom

· · · · · · · · ·

JOURNEY TO
AWAKENING

Nan C. Merrill

CONTINUUM

NEW YORK · LONDON

*Dedicated to All here on Earth
and in the heavenly realms
who have and continue to
enlighten our journey toward
Awakening with their wisdom,
love, and service.*

*Blessed are we who hear
and heed the Call.*

2002

The Continuum International Publishing Group Inc
370 Lexington Avenue, New York, NY 10017

The Continuum International Publishing Group Ltd
The Tower Building, 11 York Road, London SE1 7NX

Printed in the United States of America

Library of Congress Cataloging-in-Publication Data

Merrill, Nan C.
Lumen Christi . . . holy wisdom : journey to awakening /
Nan C. Merrill.
p. cm.
ISBN 0-8264-1386-2 (pbk.)
1. Spiritual life—Meditations.   2. Spiritual life—Catholic Church.
I. Title.

BV4501.3.M47   2002
248.3—dc21   2001056188

Preface

Lumen Christi . . . Holy Wisdom could not have been written without several *major* integrating threads along the road to awakening consciousness. The tapestry of my life—like most lives—has been woven with dark strands of pain and loss intermingled with pastels of peace and harmony, earth tones of groundedness and strength, and the bright, primary colors that bring joy to life and the energy to serve. That you may better understand the imperatives within the meditations, I offer the bare bones of these threads which have brought bountiful blessings of the Mystery and continue to enrich, strengthen, and guide my life. I pray that they will be of some blessing to all who choose to read and pray these meditations.

BEGINNING TO AWAKEN: In 1968, while rearing five young children as a Navy wife, after months of rote, unconscious early morning meditation on one particular star (though, at that time, I didn't even know the word "meditation")—a silent Cry out to the universe—I awakened one morning enveloped in LOVE . . . a state of pure Grace that lasted for ten days and set me on the Journey to awakening. Little did I know the toll of loss, pain, and suffering that this road would entail. Yet, once embarked, there was no turning back.

FACING FEAR: Within two years of being blessed by Love, I began an eight-year process of facing my fears with a counselor, *par excellence,* who encouraged and supported my inner growth toward wholeness. As I faced each fear catalyzed by inner and outer life experiences, I slowly realized that each fear faced released an energy that became transformed into a greater capacity for love. Many years later when I was held up at gunpoint and felt not an adrenal rush, but utter compassion, I knew that fear no longer enslaved me.

BEING LED BY THE SPIRIT: As I awakened and became freer to express love, I noted decisions in my life were less rational and more intuitively guided by the Spirit of Love. After discerning that I was to enter nurses' training, where I learned body systems, care-giving, and leadership (though I balked mightily), I was led to The Foundation For Religion and Mental Health, a two-year program where various psychologies were emphasized and where I also learned the crucial lesson of standing strong in my own inner values. After graduating, I was offered the opportunity to help found, coordinate, experience, assist in its direction, and, eventually, to become an adviser to another two-year program, The Guild For Spiritual Guidance. After these years of training and practice, I had developed the knowledge to give birth to a spiritual bookstore in the Berkshires of Massachusetts. Then, answering a lifelong concern for social justice, with the bookstore in a friend's capable hands, I went to serve as a lay volunteer at St. Agnes Church in the heart of Detroit. When the church was closed, I lived alone for four wondrous years on twenty-four acres in the woods near Lake Huron. There, I became so immersed in Nature that I knew moments of experiencing the Oneness, the interbeing of Creation. All of these years, balanced by service and simply being, were endowed with guidance, inner council, comfort, awakening more fully to the Unseen Realm of Love, and continued leadings by the Spirit—directly, through family, friends, new acquaintances, books, and life experiences.

ABANDONMENT TO LOVE: During a retreat about twenty years ago, I was introduced to Charles de Foucauld's "Prayer of Abandonment" . . . a prayer that continues to be the prayer of my heart. Slightly adapted with inclusive language, I pray:

> *Beloved of my heart,*
> *I abandon myself into your hands;*
> *do with me what You will.*
> *Whatever You may do, I thank You:*
> *I am ready for all, I accept all.*
> *Let only your will be done in me,*
> *and in all your creatures—*
> *I wish no more than this, my Friend.*
>
> *Into your hands, I commend my soul;*
> *I offer it to You with all the love of my heart,*
> *for I love You and so need to give myself,*
> *to surrender myself into your hands,*
> *without reserve,*
> *and with boundless confidence,*
> *for You are the Heart of my heart,*
>   *the Life of my life.*

Early on, I choked on varying phrases of the prayer starting with "Father, I abandon . . .", which was all too reminiscent of fearful, critical, judgmental authorities in my life's experience. "I am ready for all"—who me? My expectations were that all would be taken from me or I'd be asked to go where I'd rather not go. Yet, little by little, I began to live into the words, the intent, the surrender. I came to understand the mystery of "becoming the prayer," how, in a sense, a prayer can begin to pray in us. During the years of facing the labyrinth of fears, one of my deepest terrors was of being abandoned. Imagine my delight the day I recognized that to CHOOSE to abandon myself into the Hands and Heart of the Beloved, the One I could ALWAYS trust, completed the healing of that lifetime fear. I knew with every cell in my body that I, we, are never alone . . . never abandoned by Love.

SILENCE: During my time in Detroit, St. Agnes's priest, Father Edward Farrell, invited individuals from the city and the suburbs to gather together in silence to pray over the concerns of the city and the world: a contemplative community at large. Out of these days of silent prayer, the monthly newsletter *Friends of Silence* was birthed and has grown from forty to more than 5,300 subscribers over the years. To experience the efficacy of silence, to be connected to individuals who choose to spend time in silence and solitude, and to be blessed with the inward fruits of the Silence in a world filled with noise pollution, violence, and injustice continues to be a pure gift . . . and, surely, blesses the world.

LUMEN CHRISTI . . . HOLY WISDOM: Finally, I have been blessed to have received two astonishing, numinous photographs, that I yearn to share with many. The image I call Holy Wisdom was given to me by a friend when I opened the New Spirit Bookstore on the day designated as the Birth of Mary, September 8. The image appeared when processed in the United States on the film of a tourist who was simply photographing the outer door and architecture of a Coptic church north of Cairo in Egypt: the area where the Holy Family is said to have gone when fleeing Herod.

While on a silent retreat, after a year awaiting a word or phrase to use in Centering Prayer, two words spontaneously came to me one day in the chapel: LUMEN CHRISTI. At the same time, the meditations for this book began to emerge—almost as imperatives. A few days after returning home, another friend called and told me about an image of Christ she had been sent. Her friend, Lunita D'Arcy, had a sister, Marinka Salazar, in Chile, whose newborn son was in the hospital and not expected to live. Family and friends from far and near prayed, and offered distant healing. The next day, baby Christian pulled the tubes away and began to breathe normally. Later, when Lunita visited Marinka in Chile, they went to a church in the Andes to give thanks and took pictures of the chapel afterward to remember the occasion. When Lunita's film was developed in the United States, the Christ image that I now call Lumen Christi (Light of Christ) was imposed over the altar on one of the photos . . . a visitation unaware. As I continued to pray the meditations into written form, I had before me framed, enlarged prints of the two images. As each meditation emerged, it felt incomplete without the ending mantra, LUMEN CHRISTI . . . HOLY WISDOM, as a song of praise, a benediction, or an affirming Amen.

The writing of *Lumen Christi . . . Holy Wisdom* has been blessing in myriad ways. To become more aware of and to share the Eternal, Ineffable Mystery of life and death present with us through every season of our lives, ever offering Divine Hints for our Awakening to heightened consciousness has become a passion. I feel compelled to express what I have garnered on the spiritual road as my grain-of-sand service. I have learned that the more we abandon ourselves into our Divine Heritage as co-birthers with the Divine Architect, the more we live with joy, peace, and fulfillment, able to offer our lives in loving Service for the healing, sustenance, and divinization of the world. Intuitively, I know that *now* is the time for a great Spirit-quake, a giant leap in consciousness, already underway and opening wide the many hearts now being prepared to respond with enthusiasm to the Call.

Follow
your
heart-song:

your work
and
life's joy
will flow
as one
in the
service
of
Love.

Wisdom abides in deep recesses of the heart;
          who is at home to receive Her?
O friends, do not hide from Her grace;
          silent be, listen well
     as She bestows inspiration
                    to lighten your way,
          to guide you on life's pathway.
Recognize and follow the unique gifts
                    given unto you;
          remain steadfast
                    with Wisdom at your side.
Those who hear and heed the inner promptings
                    of their heart,
     become attuned to the Universal Song.

     Lumen Christi . . . Holy Wisdom.

Behold
Beauty:

bask
in the
diversity
of
Creation!

Blessed Divine Guest within heart's
                    Sacred Chapel,
          You birth us into two lives:
                    the inner, the outer
                    the worldly, the divine;
          Mirrors that bear witness
                    one to the Other.
Growth garnered in the school
          of the opposites
          diminishes separation:
                    union ends duality.
Like the tree with myriad branches,
          each unique leaf is divine,
                    united in diversity!
Holy, holy, holy is all of Creation!
          Guard well the Pearl: beautiful
                    Treasure of your heart.

          Lumen Christi . . . Holy Wisdom.

Love
is
the
root
of
Life
that
unites
all.

As dry leaves fall into compost,
winter seeds gestate
in fertile hearts,
and spring gives birth anew
for summer's ripening of the soul.
Glory to the One in all, the all in One.
Don we now our spiritual apparel:
Love and Light
a holy life
building, sustaining deep roots,
strength for seasons to come.
What in life can remain hidden
or not be attained?
Seeds of unlimited potential lie dormant;
nourish them and flourish.
Awaken to new Life!
Loving service answers many prayers.

Lumen Christi . . . Holy Wisdom.

See
the world
as
part
of yourself
and
you
will care
for it
with
Love.

Storms threaten, blights bring disease,
    like temptations that test the soul.
        Be mindful!
Wounded worlds need care for healing:
        Choose life!
    Engender Beauty and blessing!
Souls require nourishment to thrive:
    freedom, compassion, wholeness,
        integrity of heart!
        Silent be.
Aspire to a holy life of service,
    an expression of your gifts
        freely shared,
    and know joy.
Creativity blossoms in Love's Light.
    Be still and know.

Lumen Christi . . . Holy Wisdom.

Co-creation:

hidden goal
of
every
heart
that
satisfies
the
soul's
yearning.

To judge another is to see ourselves:
    fear lurking in shadows
                mirrored darkly!
Do not run! Call upon the Holy One
              and fear not!
Face your fears with Love in day's light.
    Each fear faced opens the door
             to receive more love.
    Forgiveness frees the wounded soul.
Listen deeply to others and encourage
           their aspirations
    by word, by deed, or in deep silence.
Live in a way that draws peace, beauty,
          harmony, and justice
    toward others and all of creation.
Become an ambassador of peace through
          loving service.

Lumen Christi . . . Holy Wisdom.

Calm and serene
Listen!

Whisperings
of the
Divine Guest
are heard
in open
receptive
hearts.

The Holy City beyond the sun beckons all
to enter into the Chapel
of Crystal Light
wherein abides the Universal Heart.
Listen in the silence for Spirit's Voice
guiding your soul
for service in the great renewal,
the new creation, the citadel of
Love here on Earth.
All are welcome together as One!
Listen, attune, and heed the inner Voice
of Love.
For in sacred Silence, we open ourselves
to Wisdom,
to ever deepening communion with
the Source of all creation.

Lumen Christi . . . Holy Wisdom.

Respect diversity
honor unity:

we
are all
One
in the
Eye
of
Love.

As we welcome into our awareness
the Oneness of humanity,
the interbeingness of All,
A new creativity will flourish
around the world;
justice, harmony, and beauty
will prevail in all walks of life.
Humankind will interact with one another,
with all of creation,
as an integral whole
with unity blessing diversity.
Aligned with our highest Essence,
the New Creation will be birthed
on Earth.
Blessed are you who unite
in this great Work!

Lumen Christi . . . Holy Wisdom.

Eternal Beloved,
in
your nature
we come
to know
our nature:

Fire!

Breathe in us, O Breath of Life,
strengthening and lifting
our spirits
as we awaken from our long sleep.
Be not afraid! For the Beloved's Light
is ever present;
the heart's hearth is fed
with the Fire of Love.
Naught can dampen a flaming heart ever
stoked and attended
with perserverance and care.
Free yourself from outmoded patterns;
add your voice, your service,
to build harmoniously in accordance
with the Divine Blueprint!
Welcome the dawn of a new millennium!

Lumen Christi . . . Holy Wisdom.

A
sacred breath
radiating
Love
unifies
the
divine web
of life.

Any broken part
affects
all
of
Creation.

Awaken, friends, to the Divine Radiance
  enshrined in the Inner Chapel
     of your heart;
Here your soul reflects the beauty
    of life offered in service to
      Love's Plan.
With radical trust, know every need
     will be amply supplied
  as you breathe in harmony
      with the Cosmic Song!
Time spent in the great Silence
     will serve you well . . .
  surprising you with deep peace
     and gentle joy.

Lumen Christi . . . Holy Wisdom.

You are
the
Fire of Love!

Since
You
created us
we share
in the
Fire of Love!

Scorn not the ebb and flow,
　　　　the seasons of your life.
　　Tame not the passion
　　　　　　　of the Inner Fire!
Let not the vicissitudes of worldly
　　　　　　ways and values
　　dissipate gifts that you alone
　　　　　are given to share.
Unite your voice, your heart's song,
　　with the Universal Symphony
　　　　　　　of Love!
Blessed are those souls who awaken,
　　who know the boundless joy
　　of co-birthing in concert
　　　　with the Divine Conductor!
　　　　　Silent be . . . and see.

Lumen Christi . . . Holy Wisdom.

In silence
learn
to give
of yourself
forgive others
live
with gratitude.
Then,
you need
not seek
inner peace:

Peace will find you!

Be not concerned that your gift
         may seem so small;
      your grain of sand may become
           the pearl.
Stray not from the pathway of Truth,
    the truth of the Inner Being;
    therein lies joy, fulfillment,
       and true humility.
Be grateful for all that is given;
    your needs will be met—
             and more,
    as Wisdom's Voice is heard
      throughout the lands.
Blessed are those whose hearts are open!
    Listening, they hear Wisdom's Voice
      whispering to their soul.

    Lumen Christi . . . Holy Wisdom.

Injustice
of any kind
is
NOT
a
human right.

Beloved of all hearts, You call us
to become agents of reconciliation
in this, our broken world;
To live according to our divine birthright:
as witnesses to the power
of light over darkness,
of love over fear,
of awakening over a robot life.
Let us humbly acknowledge our arrogance
as a people and a nation;
let us make reparation through sharing
our resources wherever needed.
Let us embrace self-sacrifice over greed,
and co-operation over competition.
Enliven our hearts, O Merciful Healer,
and guide us
as we hasten to repair the world
offering ourselves into Your Hands,
our hearts into Your Heart.

Lumen Christi . . . Holy Wisdom.

Through
Love and Light
all-embracing
love
and
unlimited
eternal
creativity
are
One.

New energy from on high penetrates
the Earth,
quickening the heart while sifting
weeds of old growth.
Open wide your heart's door!
Breathe in serenity; exhale peace
and harmony.
Peace is a double blessing that radiates
inward as a life-giving force,
and flows outward
as gift
to the world.
Let go of yesteryear's dogmas!
Rise above material temptations:
power and riches of the few
belong to another age.
Wisdom's way is Creation's way.
Love silence.
Here the Door opens.

Lumen Christi . . . Holy Wisdom.

To
love another
is
to see
the face
of
the Beloved
mirroring
your
own.

The hero's journey is not an easy path;
                yet great is the fulfillment:
beauty, honor, and love bestowed
                within the Heart Chalice.
Shed outmoded thought-forms; and, embrace
                more life-giving, creative ways.
                        Reach for the stars!
        Dare to follow your heart's song!
You are the future of planet Earth:
            create harmony and balance within.
Love is the Conductor of our lives;
            be like members of a fine orchestra
                with all eyes seeing as One.
Keep your inner eye single, focused
                only on Love; thus
      will the Great Conductor inspire
        and guide the music
           of your life.
Then, whatever you offer in loving
              service,
    will be returned to you
              in full measure.

Lumen Christi . . . Holy Wisdom.

Mercy
is
at the
heart
of
Hope
and
Love.

Beloved of my heart, hasten to help me;
　　　forget not this weary sojourner.
　　　　　A storm is brewing!
　　　Hide me as an eagle hides her young;
　　　　　fear paralyzes and illusions
　　　　　　　foster doubt.
Your Word abates worldly whirlwinds,
　　　　　and silences inner turmoil.
　　　With You, fear has no home.
Light casts out shadows of ignorance;
　　　a visible sign of your
　　　　　Unseen Presence.
　　　Remember! No one is ever alone!
Call upon the companioning presences
　　　of the heavenly realm.
　　　　　Express the light you are!

　　　Lumen Christi . . . Holy Wisdom.

Silence
will
unite
you
to
your
relationship
with
All.

Eons of walking in darkness are ending
       as you awaken to Oneness of being,
         the unity of all souls:
Your beginning and ending are one!
         Alpha and Omega recalled:
      past, present, and future wedded
           in no-time.
You are returning Home to re-discover
      your unique room in the Divine Plan,
      your blessing mission of service.
         You are not alone.
         Let the gentle Voice heard in the silence
          lead you on.
Be still. Listen to the heartbeat
         of Love.
      Deep silence will speak to your soul.

Lumen Christi . . . Holy Wisdom.

Every
crisis
in life
is
a call
to
healing
and
harmony.

Loving service rendered with integrity
    teaches multitudes in darkness,
       those who still sleep,
    far faster than books or lectures.
Do not condemn, nor condone, ignorance.
    Prisons are but reflections
      of society's shadowed sins;
    they do not heal deep wounds.
Those who knowingly broadcast ignorance
      are evil;
    beware of their insidious influence!
    The blood of millions soaks the earth.
Earth's response will teach humility:
    will She shake us off into oblivion,
    or will we embrace Love and Wisdom
      united to heal Her wounds
    and render humanity's healing as well?
    The bell has sounded.
    NOW, the wake-up call!

Lumen Christi . . . Holy Wisdom.

Change
your
thinking
and
your
reality
will also
change.

We are not alone. The unseen Realm—
     those who have gone before us,
     angels, and guides—live among us,
     ever ready to respond to our call.
Awaken! Know the splendor of co-creating
          in the Divine Plan
       with the Beloved Community
     as the world groans in the birth
           of a new dawn.
Simply ask. You will smile with gratitude
       at Their ready response.
The days of those who understand
       will flow like a pure river;
     obstacles cannot impede their way
       to the Source.
Rejoice in the unique consciousness
     that you are.
Live your life to the fullest.
Blessed are you who walk this road:
     earth angels in disguise.

     Lumen Christi . . . Holy Wisdom.

World peace
will follow
as we
find
peace
within
our own
souls.

Sometimes You seem to abandon us,
      to hide, though we know
      You make your Home in our hearts.
What does it mean that You tease
         our souls with murmurs,
      that we struggle,
      that we so often fail to hear
      and heed your Will?
How do we break through old habits
      and dark, fear thoughts
        that separate and divide?
Penetrate our spirits and awaken us
      with your Light,
      O Spirit of Truth.
      Illumine our souls with insight.
Peace among the nations is possible.
      Love will show the way.
      Who will heed the Call?

Lumen Christi . . . Holy Wisdom.

Love's
warm and gentle
Presence
resides
within
you.

Be still
and
rest in
Love's embrace.

"Were you to gaze upon Me, O friends,
the Light, like the sun,
would blind you;
your spiritual eyes are yet weak.
Weep not, nor grow weary of the journey:
love is its own reward,
and time is your friend.
Progress is assured as you confront
the fears lurking within,
fears that trouble the spirit
with doubt and illusion.
Call upon the angels and guides I send
to awaken you from inertia to joy.
Let deep, silent centering prayer within
enlighten your way."
Divine Love and Light are mirrors
of silence in which
all of creation is reflected.

Lumen Christi . . . Holy Wisdom.

Time
spent
in
holy
solitude
can
silence
the
noisy world
ever at work
in our
minds.

Many are the routes along the way;
　　　　choose the narrow path,
　　the simple road that opens
　　　　　　the Heart's door,
　　　　the abode of the Divine Guest.
Out of solitude and deepening meditation
　　　　　　　in the Silence
　　Wisdom whispers to your spirit:
　　　　Surrender!
　　　　　　　The Treasure is within you.
Stay awake! Steep is the inward pathway
　　　　to clear and lofty thoughts.
Take the staff of mindfulness with you
　　　　　　on the ascent
　　　　to higher vibrations of Light:
　　Awakened consciousness! Resurrection!
Mirrored reflections of Divine Love, Will,
　　　　　　Power, and Light.

　　Lumen Christi . . . Holy Wisdom.

Deep
Silence
of the heart
opens the
doorway
to
peace, joy
and
a
life
of
service.

Silence is a doorway
        into the heart of reality;
        to cultivate a silent heart
            is to discover your deepest truth.
Being true to yourself in every moment,
      the universe conspires to bring
              fulfillment.
When your soul's deep yearning
      and spiritual destiny become One,
         united in Being,
Balance, peace, and harmony are achieved;
      you have awakened to Love's call.
The penetrating Spirit and receptive Soul
          wedded in a Sacred Marriage.
              Behold!
          All is made new!

Lumen Christi . . . Holy Wisdom.

Listen
attentively
to how
YOU
are being
called
to
Serve.

Spirit is the foundation of our lives.
　　　To partner with Love and Light
　　　　　enkindles the inner spark
　　　　　　　of divinity:
　　　We awaken! We learn to discern and honor
　　　　　　　the sacredness of all life.
To help awaken individuals lulled to sleep
　　　　　by a world that fosters
　　　　　　　　　　ignorance and illusion
　　　calls for dedicated souls who live
　　　　　the principles of sharing, justice,
　　　　　　　love, and community.
Who will hear the inner call now beating
　　　　　within their hearts
　　　　　and respond, ready to serve?
Who will enthusiastically unite
　　　　　with individuals of all nations
　　　for nothing less
　　　than the healing, the renewal,
　　　　　of our world?

　　　Lumen Christi . . . Holy Wisdom.

All
loves
reflect
the
One Love
and
ultimately
lead to
that
Love.

Beloved are you who seek the Truth
and trust your Inner Being:
home of the Divine Guest.
Seeing with compassionate eyes,
you uphold the good,
you strengthen the weak;
You wear courage and understanding
as shields before ignorance.
Love is the great healer;
the unjust are cleansed in its power;
they are drawn to Love like moths
to a flame;
They are burned and refined by a Fire
not quenched by water.
Awaken, O friends, to the Fire of Love!

Lumen Christi . . . Holy Wisdom.

"You
are the
light
of the
world."

SHINE!

Awakened to the light that radiates
in and through you,
your very presence affirms
the light in others.
Switch on! Activate the light you are.
Become a beacon of light!
Those whose hearts are open, gain
soul-sight and rejoice,
their eternal yearning satisfied:
free from the limitations imposed
by fears and doubt,
their capacity for Love expands.
Light-bearers welcome and encourage them:
new points of light in action,
serving as co-birthers
in the Divine Plan.

Lumen Christi . . . Holy Wisdom.

You
are loved
beyond
measure!

Receive
and
radiate
Love beams
to the
world.

Marked is the path of every soul;
        follow your own unique
                    Heart-song;
        attune to the melody of joy.
Meditate! Center your prayer on Love!
        Cultivate the heart's garden
                    with Silence:
As the soul is nurtured, thus does
        the Sacred Chapel within shine.
A Radiant Heart filled with Love
        teaches without teaching.
Gathered together, Love's symphony
        penetrates hearts
                    paralyzed by fear.
        Come!
                Become an instrument
                    of the Divine Conductor!
                Join in the Universal Song!

        Lumen Christi . . . Holy Wisdom.

Join
in
and
express
your joy
in the
cosmic
dance
of
Life!

A joy-filled heart creates peace,
                              order, and harmony:
              for the song of the soul is a joy
                    that calms inner storms,
                    and beams light into the darkness.
              A smile lifts at least two hearts.
A jubilant heart overflows with gratitude,
                    initiates selfless service,
              beats in harmony with the universe,
                    and blesses the world.
Cultivate within yourself a sacred garden
                    of silence with
              blossoms of beauty to share.
Joy and justice are sisters
                    that lighten the heart
                    and point the way.

       Lumen Christi . . . Holy Wisdom.

Breathing
mindfully
helps
you
enter
deep
inner
silence.

Breathe deeply amidst the beauties
of nature;
absorb vibrations unsullied by
pollution and cosmopolitan ways.
Breathing mindfully brings balance into
your life;
strength is gained through the
Breath of Life!
Remember: breath is your life's companion!
And, as you limit your breath, you limit
life itself.
Befriend silence: a balm to your soul.
As you breathe in silence,
your ear attunes to Spirit.
You will understand the eagle.
Breathe deeply! Breathe life!

Lumen Christi . . . Holy Wisdom.

Awaken
to
the
light
of
greater
awareness
within
you.

Fill us with the radiance of your Light,
                    O Light Divine!
Uphold the Light that your inner light
        may illumine fear-filled hearts.
Even a life filled with fragrant roses
        must endure many earthly thorns.
Yet, with true understanding, our hearts
                    and minds
        become open to harmlessness.
We become beneficent presences
                    where're we happen to be:
Building blocks for the Divine Architect.
        Light comes with each new dawn.
        yield to the Light within;
                become a chalice of light
                for the world!

        Lumen Christi . . . Holy Wisdom.

Create
in
your heart
an altar
of
beauty
and
silence.

We are all sojourners on the path
                    to enlightenment,
            the work of transformation,
        the pilgrimage to awakened consciousness.
In the womb of silence, we are given
            profound insights,
        activating the union of soul
            and spirit,
                    the earthly and divine.
Here compassion, wisdom, justice,
                        and true service
            awaken in heart and mind:
            calls to action.
Here we learn to love, to co-create
        with the vibrant world of Spirit.
            Here we find Life!

    Lumen Christi . . . Holy Wisdom.

May
the
Light
you bear
illumine
the face
of the
Beloved
in
everyone
you
see.

Ask that your consciousness
        be filled with Light;
    ask to be illumined to follow
        the path of simplicity
    with integrity and inner sight.
Inspired by Divine Light and Love
        you begin to express Divine Will
            in action:
    thus will your journey be eased,
        joy will nest in your heart.
Awakening to the indwelling Divine Guest,
        Loving Companion Presence
            of your heart,
    family, friends, and strangers alike
        are greeted with compassion.
A greater state of awareness being aroused,
        you recognize the interconnectedness
            of everything and everyone:
            the unity of diversity.

Lumen Christi . . . Holy Wisdom.

Die
daily
and
begin
to
live
with
wonder.

To die daily opens the gateway
        to sacred spontaneity,
   to a greater life of freedom
      and fulfillment.
A humbled heart is a key that unlocks
   the prison doors holding us
     in bondage:
   releasing us into Love's hands,
   strengthening us to face the fears
     and doubts that bind us.
Walk the path of devotion and love;
   awaken to your unseen,
       yet ever-present,
   spiritual guides and companions.
To die to all that veils our deepest truth,
   whether intellectually, emotionally,
    physically, or spiritually
   is but an entrance into a more
     wondrous and vibrant world.
     Kneel down and ascend!

Lumen Christi . . . Holy Wisdom.

Wisdom
reveals
the
miraculous
in
everyday
living
as we
open to
the
eternal
NOW.

Divine abundance, the natural order
                    of the universe,
    is rendered ineffective in the face
            of greed, fear, and ignorance.
Beware: aggression, arrogance, and self-
            serving assumptions proliferate,
        hindering the union of heart and mind,
            will and wisdom, understanding
                    and love:
All central to the birth of the New Dawn.
Awaken, O humanity! Awaken, O nations!
        Waste not our Divine resources
                in nature, in our hearts.
Awakening, Wisdom engenders soul awareness,
        worldly integrity, and Divine
            understanding in thought,
                word, and deed.
Experience the joy of co-creation in service
        with the life-force of Spirit!

    Lumen Christi . . . Holy Wisdom.

True
Beauty
is a
radiance
emanating
from
the
soul.

Why grope in darkness when the Beloved
abides within your heart?
Chaos transformed becomes beauty,
a dancing joy.
Awaken! When the heart has opened
the door to love,
the inner eye sees with soul-sight.
Lonely are those who have yet to realize
the light of love.
You are created for love! More precious
than all the world's treasures
is the heart alight with love!
Once you experience the Beloved
of your heart,
ever present at each moment,
you will never again feel alone.

Lumen Christi . . . Holy Wisdom.

Love
will
stretch
the heart
until
it
breaks
open.
Then,

LIGHT!

The power of Universal Love, the force
        of Awakened Consciousness,
    frees the soul to express itself as
        a healing radiance of blessing,
            a channel of light.
Abandon yourself to the Divine Will
    thus will you be enabled to serve
        with vitality, ease, and strength.
Only your will power can surrender to the
            ultimate Will Power.
        Wait on Wisdom's Will!
    Place all in the Pure Light within!
Surrendered into the Heart of Love
    with your yearnings fully revealed,
        there is no separation:
            only One.

    Lumen Christi . . . Holy Wisdom.

Silence
devotion
forgiveness
and
prayer
are
gateways
to the
Great Healer:

LOVE.

Tears are nourishment that well up
in loving hearts
healing and awakening the soul
to Love.
Much will be given in the silence,
your closet of prayer.
Fiery leadings of the Spirit burst forth
as insight, vision, and purpose;
intuitively you perceive the world
with Wisdom's clarity.
You become an active participant
in the healing and harmonizing
of our blue-green jewel:
planet Earth.
What greater purpose than to reawaken,
to serve consciously, lovingly,
in the Divine Plan:
To experience the sacred in every soul
here on earth
and in the unseen realm
ever with us!

Lumen Christi . . . Holy Wisdom.

May
the
service
you render
reflect
the
deepest
aspirations
of
your
heart.

Remain vigilant! Tend the flame, the
                    Divine Spark that
                nurtures and guides your way!
Not for drugery of duty do you awaken;
        rather to delight: to dance and play
                within creation's wonders.
Enlightened souls know the joy and power
                    of humble service
            offered freely, lovingly,
                in harmony with the Universal Song.
When the flame shines brightly,
            who remembers the darkness?
                Remain vigilant!
Even in difficult moments, remember
                to be mindful:
            You are never alone.

        Lumen Christi . . . Holy Wisdom.

The
Divine
Breath
Breath of Life
contains
all
of
life.

Breathe in deeply the Breath of Divine
Love,
breathe out fully the breath
of peace and harmony.
Freedom resides in the Breath of Life.
Shallow breathing dams the fluidity
of aspiration and creativity.
Fullness of breath in an emptied mind
becomes a Cosmic Energizer
that revitalizes organs, senses,
spirit, and will to action.
Nurture yourself with feasts of breath
in silence and solitude:
healing and holiness become the gift.
Each inhalation and exhalation interconnects
with the Universal Breath:
The play of breath with Breath,
mutual communion.
Breathe deeply the breath of Life!

Lumen Christi . . . Holy Wisdom.

In
silence
drink deeply
from
the
inner
cup
of
Wisdom.

Ego desires do not easily surrender;
  long is the road to the awakening
   freedom
   of utter abandonment to Love,
   Light, and Life!
The cross of pain and loss as the false
    self dies opens into
  a holy crucible of Love's Flame.
Here, darkness does not overwhelm;
  but becomes a silence,
   a soothing womb of rest,
  that dazzles with Unseen Light.
Seek Wisdom. She will ease, comfort,
   and strengthen you on each step
   of the journey.
Fear not! Embrace the Mystery of Love
   ever loving you!

  Lumen Christi . . . Holy Wisdom.

The
world's
future
depends
upon
our
awakening
to
Love's
Call.

Crucial for human life, only love
　　　can enflame the Divine Spark
　　　　　within your heart.
Let devotion ever be a call
　　　　　until with full measure
　　　you can bow down and kiss
　　　　　　　　the ground
With tears of undying compassion
　　　for all of creation
　　　and those who dwell therein.
Receive the glad tidings of Love
　　　that permeate the world amidst
　　　　　suffering, pain, and chaos.
Surrender to the guiding Hand,
　　　the merciful Heart,
　　　　　of the Beloved:
　　　connecting Source of All.

　　　Lumen Christi . . . Holy Wisdom.

Angels
rejoice
as
we
befriend
their
companioning
presence.

When wrestling with a wounding angel,
struggle mightily:
your very way of being
may be at stake.
Life as you know it may well melt away:
yet a shattered heart is opened
to the Light.
Grieve the loss! Cry out the pain!
But linger not long.
Sorrow is but the shadow side
of joy. Remember!
Tears refresh the heart-soil like
dew drops nourishing the earth
at dawn.
Whether slow and gentle or harsh
and filled with anguish,
angelic awakening portends new life.
Seize the challenge! Receive the blessings
of new birth, awakened consciousness!
Resurrection!

Lumen Christi . . . Holy Wisdom.

The
darkness
disappears
in the
Light
of
Love's
flame.

Awakening opens the inner doorway
to intuitions of Holy Wisdom's way:
the inner Laws of Love written
upon the heart.
Awakening reveals hidden potentials,
the way of Lumen Christi:
the penetrating power of knowledge
on the humble path.
Hold high the torch of Light, that
what dwells in darkness may be
seen, faced, and embraced.
Thus, hidden treasures begin to shine;
redemption is at work.
Aspire to become a beacon of Light!
a chalice of Love!

Lumen Christi . . . Holy Wisdom.

Be
mindful
of the
fruit
the
thought-seeds
you sow
will
bear.

Arise! Become a rebel for the Spirit!
Let not worldly wars and woes
paralyze your aspiration
to unite in the birth of a new dawn.
Discouragement and despair burden
the heart:
dark thoughts often lead to
deadly deeds.
Dive deeply into the Cosmic Ocean of Love!
Here harmony, beauty, peace, truth,
and inspiration reign:
needed for the healing and repair
of this wondrous world.
Become a beneficial rebel in the service
of Love and Light!
Look within the Silence:
Divine Hints will set you on the pathway
to new Life offering guidance,
comfort, and strength
for the journey.

Lumen Christi . . . Holy Wisdom.

Attitude
strengthens
or
weakens
aspirations
of the
heart.

Whatever-comes-along faith is like leaves
blowing in the wind,
while
Giving one's power to worldly authority
is faith denied, a soul devoid
of freedom.
Awakened faith lives by the Law written
on each heart that hears and heeds
the Voice of Silence.
One's own unique and authentic faith
becomes expressed with utter
integrity in action.
Aspire to know the Truth that awakens
the heart,
the Truth that sets you free!

Lumen Christi . . . Holy Wisdom.

Beyond
the
luminous
Veil
is
utter
unity.

Your hidden life within the heart womb
       is a witness to the world
             when its light is united
              to Love.
Be still and rest in the Infinite Ocean
            of Love's Mercy.
Deep prayer in solitude and silence
            is a purifying crucible
       that refines the soul and bestows
             gifts of the Spirit.
Enter into the inner hermitage,
        and be still;
                rest in this holy, silent space.
Here you awaken to your true self,
      that which you were before birth:
         your Eternal Essence.
      Let Silence become your teacher.

      Lumen Christi . . . Holy Wisdom.

The
gateway
to
heaven
is
wherever
you
are.

Awaken and attune to Wisdom's Voice
　　ever with you in the heart-womb;
　　　　wise are those who hear,
　　　　who surrender to Her Call.
A question arises: What can I do
　　to render back to Love
　　　　　　a gratitude beyond words?
An answer is heard: Become the bread
　　　　　　of Life,
　　kneaded thoroughly until pliant
　　　　in the Hands of Love:
Nourishment for hungry souls waiting
　　　　to be filled, so that they, too,
　　　　become the bread of Life for others.
Listen to the sounds of silence:
　　　　the language of the heart.
And may you ever be blessed by Beauty:
　　the song of Songs within your heart.

　　Lumen Christi . . . Holy Wisdom.

You
are
a
single blossom
in the
integral
community garden:

our planet
Earth.

Attune your soul to Creation's Beauty;
　　　contemplate her amazing abundance:
　　　an Earth Garden overflowing
　　　　　with myriad gifts of life
　　　　　to inspire, to satisfy our every need.
Bask quietly in Beauty not made by
　　　　　　　　human hands;
　　　breathe in rays of Divine Light,
　　　　　fragrance of the Beloved.
Consider the blossoms your life brings
　　　　　to the great garden of Life.
Awaken to wonders—great and small—
　　　　　sown by the Divine Gardener;
　　　humbly offer your heart in gratitude,
　　　　　　　your hands in service.
Thus does the vibrant beauty within grow.

　　　Lumen Christi . . . Holy Wisdom.

The
spiritual
life
calls us
to
selfless
service
and
Love.

Light-bearers are needed in every walk
                    of life as dark forces ply
                their crafty trade.
As pilgrims facing eternity on this brief
                    earthly sojourn,
            awakening to the Light eases
                    the return trip Home.
Breathe in the pure Light of truth
                    while you may;
        a vessel of Light still shines
                    even when cracked or broken.
When the call comes, blessed are those
                who respond without fear;
        Love is the helping hand sent
                    to guide each soul,
                to heal wounds of the heart.
Silent be and listen! Welcome Wisdom's
            gentle hints and walk in peace.

        Lumen Christi . . . Holy Wisdom.

A
tranquil
soul
lives
in a
vibrant
field
of
peace.

How can we strive for peace with another
 if we are not in harmony and accord
  within our own being?
When we are like a swarm of bees, too busy,
 quarrelsome, distracted,
  when we are filled with anger,
   doubts, and fear,
    with whom we can be at peace?
Awaken! Find a flower-filled field
      and be still.
Observe the bees following their natural
 call: pollinating, all the while
  imbibing in sweet nectar:
   creation-gifts for other creatures.
Until we learn to live with harmony, hope,
 and loving-balance
  within our own hearts,
How can there be peace among the nations?

 Lumen Christi . . . Holy Wisdom.

Die
to your
false
self
and
be born
to
a
new
life
of
joy.

Amidst the crowded cities, the daily
                tasks of life,
few there are who know peace,
                the "felicitude" of solitude.
Myriad follow the lure of luxury,
                a frantic search for pleasure;
Soul requirements call for silence,
                sacred time alone in heart space
                and stillness.
A balanced life engenders harmony of body,
                mind, emotions, and soul
in work, prayer, and recreation
                in the outer world,
re-creation in silence and solitude,
                inwardly at home with Divine Love.
Let Wisdom teach and illuminate the way!
                Cherish your times in sacred space
                with silence and solitude.

Lumen Christi . . . Holy Wisdom.

Greet
your
daily
disciplines
with
open heart
and
enthusiasm.

Sully not the inner Chapel of Love with
                impure thoughts, unholy deeds.
                        Awaken!
Attending daily to silence, sacred readings,
                dedicated service, and prayer
            keeps the mind attentive, the heart
                attuned to Love: a balanced life.
Find serenity in the light of Truth,
                the wisdom of discerned action.
            Know truth, speak truth, live truth
                and, "the truth will set you free."
Through life itself come daily lessons
                of enlightenment.
            Rest in the ever-present guidance
                of the Light, the assurance of Love.
                Let Beauty become the way;
Call upon the eternal Teacher and Counselor.

            Lumen Christi . . . Holy Wisdom.

Remain
non-attached
to life's
ups and downs:

let
gentle joy
and
inner peace
rest in
you.

What dwells in our hearts that we
　　so easily resist the good?
　　　　Our intentions fade away.
Firm resolve falters, high aspirations
　　　　grow weak
　　when distractions and desires
　　　　appear on the path.
Like butterflies flitting from flower
　　　　to flower,
　　we settle for ephemeral fancies.
Awaken! Our soul's joy is found
　　　　in friendship with the Beloved,
　　in co-creating a new future
　　　　with Love!
Envision your heart's true birthright
　　　　and set sail.

　　Lumen Christi . . . Holy Wisdom.

Beloved
of
all
hearts,
You
are
our
Home.

In the Silence, empty your mind
                of worldly concerns
        to give prayer space to grow:
Thus do you awaken to your unique Call
                to serve in the Divine Plan.
In stillness, discover Beauty, through
        the opening of your heart's eye.
For Silence, Mercy, and Beauty
                know no national boundaries;
        they cut through language, dogma,
                and enmities.
Strive for pure understanding, clarity
        of purpose; guard well the gateway
                to the Sacred Garden sown
                        with seeds of peace:
Here heartfelt prayer rises quietly
                amidst Beauty's blossoms.

        Lumen Christi . . . Holy Wisdom.

Humility
teaches:

we
are not
the
rulers
of the
universe.

Envision the future of planet Earth
                    and tremble;
          virulent is the darkness wrought
                    by human hands.
Dried and barren are hearts that succumb
                    to the quest for riches:
          greed, arrogance, injustice,
                    and illusion breed here.
                    Yet take heart!
Light-workers of the world are assembling;
                    courage, justice, truth, hope,
                    and philanthropy
          are spreading like flames
                              across a dry prairie.
Blessed are all who are prepared to answer
          the Call to serve with Love and Light.

Lumen Christi . . . Holy Wisdom.

Love
Beauty
Service:

three paths
to
wholeness
peace
and
joy.

Turn not away from the narrow path
        lest darkness overshadow the soul,
                and unholy thoughts and desires
                        rise up unbidden to
        clouding the mind, staining the heart.
Wend your way through the corridors
                        of time,
        not as passengers on a free ride
                watching the seasons pass;
Rather, steady mindfulness quickens
                the spirit, awakens the soul,
        and opens the Inner Gate that leads
                to the great Work so needed
                        in these times.
Discover the joy of helping humanity
                to reverence all Life,
        of offering your healing hands
        in the restoration of planet Earth.
Discernment and discipline will cut through
                impediments to action.

        Lumen Christi . . . Holy Wisdom.

Selfless
living
gives birth
to
peace-filled
clear
awareness:

transparency.

Fear not the evolving world: transformation
at the heart of life renewal.
Change creates tension: fear of loss;
let slow and gradual be the pace.
The Foundation Stone remains strong and true.
Needed are builders of the New Dawn
even now arising.
Manifold is the wondrous Work ahead;
progress is already underway.
Guidance and inspiration manifest to those
who listen in the silence
for the Divine Hints ever offered.
Welcome the needed change as you participate
in the Divine Plan!
Awaken to shared joy, love, beauty,
and a deep abiding peace
beyond measure.

Lumen Christi . . . Holy Wisdom.

Compassion
takes
practice
to
flow
freely
from
the
heart.

Awaken! that the dreams of the night
may bring lessons of the heart
taught by the Great Dreamer.
Night encounters in study halls seen
only in the spirit
ready the willing student to teach
in the University of Love.
Beware of idle talk, of useless hours
spent with media madness!
They weaken mind-frequencies and invite
darkness into the soul.
Facing fears, diminishing doubts,
are prerequisites
in the school of Life.
Every chosen moment spent in the Silence
readies the soul to receive
the gifts of Love.
Awaken! Prepare your Sacred Inner Being
for the priceless Pearl!

Lumen Christi . . . Holy Wisdom.

True
friendship
is
filled
with
silent
communication.

Imagine a world of unity, where everyone
      is accepted as a unique consciousness
      of equal value:
            essential to the Whole.
Dim is the light in this present world
      so afflicted with the violence of war,
           greed, injustice, oppression:
                degradation.
Recognize the Truth that flows through all,
      the interbeing of souls,
          though varied are the ways.
Let us embrace diversity as we unite
      our wills with the Divine Will:
      together we will re-create a world
          luminous with Love and Light
          radiating from each heart.

Lumen Christi . . . Holy Wisdom.

Beauty:

to
SEE
with
our
heart's eyes
opened
wide.

Surrender to the tempering of the Spirit:
strength is built through daily
disciplines and the breath;
Breathe deeply, then, the Life-giving
essence of Beauty, Love,
and Light.
Wisdom will pluck the strings
of your heart.
Burdens become beams of harmony and joy
to the light-bearing wayfarer;
share this illuminating joy
with those who still await the call
to higher awareness.
May eternal Sacred Chants ever resonate
deeply within your heart
as you add your voice
to the Universal Chorus.

Lumen Christi . . . Holy Wisdom.

Be aware:

Darkness
is
birthed
by
destructive
thinking.

Each soul is born for love and joy.
    Our Inner Radiance when,
    fully uncovered,
        shines alike
            in laughter and in sorrow.
Fears, doubts, and despair cloak joy
        like darkness blanketing the sun
            each night.
Face your fears and freedom will follow,
      dismantle doubts and loving assurance
        becomes a friend;
Dark despair diminishes as you turn
        toward the Light.
        Help is ever at hand.
    Your guardian angel awaits your call!
Dispelling the darkness, you increase hope
        in the world.
Rejoice! Humanity *is* inexorably awakening
    to the energy of Love.

Lumen Christi . . . Holy Wisdom.

Meditate
and
become
centered
in the
deep well
of
truth.

Old habits stultify soul growth;
      they are like stagnant ponds
          lacking springs of living water.
Assert your will to release each
      outworn, deadening addiction;
Courage and prayer act as magnets
      drawing life-giving energy to you
         every step of the way.
Awaken! Release of yesterday's unwise
             choices
      opens the portals to abundant life.
Call upon the sustaining power of Light,
      the comforting of Mercy,
         the leadings of Love:
      traveling companions to attend you
      on the journey to wholeness.

Lumen Christi . . . Holy Wisdom.

Be
mindful:

as
you
think
so
you
become.

See humanity awakening to new ways
of interacting with one another,
to fears being transformed
into loving relationships.
All manner of exploitation supplanted
by creative living is one hope
for our wounded world.
The Flame is lit. Sparks abound,
entering hearts prepared to spread
the fire of Love.
Deep yearnings for simplicity, beauty,
and more harmonious living
have been heard.
Those who answer the Call will know joy
and be wondrously blessed
as the Dream for Earth becomes
a reality.
Heightened awareness becomes mutual
blessing for you, the nations,
and all of the world.

Lumen Christi . . . Holy Wisdom.

Your
deepest
wound
may
become
your
greatest
gift.

Consider the hidden blessings of adversity!
    The other side of sorrow is joy.
    Draw from your own Inner Well
        nourishment for the soul.
You will find plenty to share with others.
Fertilize and cultivate the ground
        of your Being with care:
Centering prayer, silence, and simplicity
    are worthy companions as you tread
        paths leading to freedom and joy.
        Act now!
A Spirit-quake of great magnitude is
        sending out tremors: even now
    ripples are being felt throughout
        the Cosmos!
Nothing less than a complete renewal
        of Earth and Her inhabitants
        is at hand.

Lumen Christi . . . Holy Wisdom.

Live
and
rest
in
and
through
the
Light
of
the
Word.

Light dwells deep within each of us
               ready to radiate forth
      as our will freely surrenders
      in alignment with our soul's purpose.
We are here on Earth to lift and deepen
          our own awareness and that of creation:
              co-partners in the Divine Plan
      for the divinization of all creation.
Seek within and find the Source
                 of Love and Light.
      Shine in unity with all whose joy
      is to co-birth as a light
      in the world.
A new dawn is rising. Awaken! Come!
          Find your placement in the Great Work
             creating an incandescent network
                 of Light around the planet.
"Source of All, act within my being,
      that I may act in accordance
             with Thine."

Lumen Christi . . . Holy Wisdom.

Reverence
the
truth
of
your
Inner Being:

Love.

Celestial silence penetrates
          the listening ear
      not deafened by worldly clamor,
Creating in the heart a sacred space:
          an abode for Divine Love,
     a heaven blessed haven in troubled
            times.
Hallow the Inner Sanctuary, the truth
        of your being through goodness,
     kindness, and life-giving
        thoughts, words, and deeds.
Out of the silence sponsored by Authority
         from on high
     will come hope and the strength
     and courage to act and serve.
        Aspire toward awakening!
        Knock, seek, and find!

Lumen Christi . . . Holy Wisdom.

Meditation
cleanses
the
soul
and
reveals
hidden
beauty.

Luminous is the word of Truth; like
a laser beam, it cuts through
ignorance and illusion.
Lives filled with lies lead to pain
and suffering;
the face reveals but a mask
hiding shame and deception.
About face! Awaken! Never is it too late
to seek Wisdom! More precious
than gold is the rebirth
of a tortured soul.
Listen and know! In the silence, hear
your heart beating in harmony
with the Beloved's Heart,
companion of your soul.
Blessed are those who choose the Truth.
The path is made straight,
their spirit freed to soar.

Lumen Christi . . . Holy Wisdom.

True
conscience
is
the
silent
voice
of your
soul.

Listen!

Right relationships are built on firm
                 foundations;
        justice, harmony, peace, love,
                 and assurance are the bricks.
Worldly ambitions tend to separate
        individuals one from the other,
        humanity from its Divine Source.
Listen to the Voice within your soul.
        Hear the cries of the oppressed
                 and exploited.
        Injustice and violence are rampant,
Even as our hearts yearn for wholeness,
                 for freedom, light, and joy.
Let us plant seeds of justice in the
                 heart-soil
        that gardens of peace may blossom
                 throughout the world . . .
Righting relationships in harmony and love.

        Lumen Christi . . . Holy Wisdom.

When
did
you
last
thank
your
guardian
angel?

Every heart yearns for the holy,
              for deep meaning to life,
         to be touched by the wings
              of an angel.
To befriend the Sacred, to live
              in harmony and peace,
         to fulfill one's highest aspirations
              and potential requires action.
Awaken! This blessed desire is the Call!
         Much once dear to the heart
              must be cast away;
         for a vessel must be emptied
              to receive new wine:
A spirit of joy, gratitude, love, hope,
              and assurance—
         strength for the Work ahead.
To empower one another is to evoke
         unique gifts of the universal
              community: to become
         a partner in the joy of Cosmic
              co-creating!

Lumen Christi . . . Holy Wisdom.

You
are
a
pilgrim
on the
Eternal Journey
learning
to express
Love
and to
radiate
Light.

The Beloved of all Hearts dwells within,
    veiled by ego desires, fears, biases,
        illusion, and zealous worldly
            pursuits,
Yet known and welcomed by those who have
        developed heightened awareness,
    whose hearts are open and receptive.
How cumbersome is the luggage we continue
        to collect and carry
    through outmoded habits, unforgiven
      hurts, stress, and distress!
Radical simplification greatly lightens
        the journey,
    enhances daily living, and blesses
    the sojourner with wonder and joy.
The only true soul map is found within:
    ask the Inner Counselor to lead
      and guide you on the way.

Lumen Christi . . . Holy Wisdom.

Selfless
service
leads
at last
to
You,
O Beloved.

Love and service walk hand in hand:
 solutions to a world that seems
  bent on destruction.
Forgotten is Creation, sacred handiwork
  of the Divine Imagination
 for the sustenance and awakening
  consciousness of humankind.
Technology and materialism all too often
  bring blight to the world,
 filling the pockets of a few, while
  millions hunger and thirst
   in dire straights.
Responsible, effective, appropriate service
 begins in the heart, the abode
  of Divine Love.
 Light workers of the world: unite!
May the wills of many in Oneness with
   Divine Will and Mercy
 create a Love revolution
  for the re-creation of planet Earth:
  Life to us all.

Lumen Christi . . . Holy Wisdom.

Your
name
is
holy:

a
sacred
trust.

In a world filled with suffering, needed
　　　　　are compassionate listeners,
　　　healing presences, creators of beauty,
　　　　　and active workers for justice.
In peril is the human mind, seeded with
　　　　　vile vibrations of the violence,
　　　　　　trivia, and illusion
　　　sown by many media moguls, perverters
　　　　　of truth.
When weeds take over, lost are the blossoms
　　　of inspiration, discernment, peace,
　　　　　　and joy.
O, Compassionate One, You who understand
　　　　　the secrets of the heart,
　　　You who call us by name and love us,
　　　　　hear the silent cries of our souls.

　　　Lumen Christi . . . Holy Wisdom.

Recognize
the
Divine Guest
in all
you
meet
and
in all
you
do.

As the New Dawn arises unbelievable
              are the changes and challenges
              to come:
Never has the call for light-bearers,
       those who choose to serve
                     in the Divine Plan, been so great.
The de-creation of old habits, institutions,
              negative emotions, superstitions,
       and outmoded thought patterns has begun.
              Let not dark forces thwart the Plan!
Welcome the Living Community of non-physical
                     friends from the Celestial Realm
              who await your answer to the Call.
       Co-creation will become your joy!
True values of sharing, beauty, justice,
              unity, spiritual understanding,
                     integrity, and love
       shine through the underbrush
                     of old compost:
              Gold in the Service of Love.

Lumen Christi . . . Holy Wisdom.

Contemplate
the
Beauty
of your
soul
and
see
Beauty
everywhere.

Prayer is not a solo art form:
                for, we never pray alone;
        all prayers offered to the Beloved
        by whatever Name, whatever form,
Meet in the Holy Tabernacle on high,
        lifting the hearts, needs, and hopes
                of myriad souls.
Let not dark thoughts reflecting fear,
        illusion, superstition, or enmity
                pollute pure prayer intent.
A purified life dedicated to the Light
                through love and service
        shines like a rainbow through
                clear crystal.
United in prayer and purpose, individuals
                from every nation
        sowing sacred seeds of peace,
                truth, and love,
Create the power to usher in the New Dawn.
        Let us move inexorably onward toward
                the divinization of planet Earth.

Lumen Christi . . . Holy Wisdom.

Ground
your heart
and
actions
in
Wisdom
and
Love
and
awaken
to
peace.

Evil are the ways of those who exert
                    their will
    at the expense of humanity and nature.
Denying the divine birthright of all
                to love and serve,
    the joy of gifts shared and beauty
           expressed eludes them.
Their inner beings are bound, enslaved,
      in a self-made dungeon
                  of dis-ease and despair.
O, you who are not yet awake, the alarm
          has sounded!
    Be mindful of what the seeds that
        you sow will bear.
Awakened hearts rejoice at the dawn
        and sleep peacefully through
           the night.
Yet, many there are who will have much
      to answer for.
    Turn to the Light!

Lumen Christi . . . Holy Wisdom.

Awaken
to
wonder:

the
glory
of
Creation.

Strength and beauty abide in unity,
        love is expressed through sharing.
Justice and mercy are keys that unlock
                the gates to peace
        and manifest the Oneness we are.
                Awaken!
Activate these sacred seeds, and watch
        the walls of separation crumble!
Arising from the rubble are spontaneity,
                wonder, and synchronicity:
                        forerunners of joy!
Evoke and support the Seed gestating
                in the soul of another.
        Hidden beneath the heart-soil,
Love is the dynamic force to draw forth
        blossoms of beauty, flowers of Life.
        All that we love mirrors who we are.

Lumen Christi . . . Holy Wisdom.

Our
thoughts
words
and
deeds
bind us
or
free us
to
soar.

Be ever mindful that each thought
        draws to itself
    all that is visualized inwardly.
Lift your heart and aspirations;
      behold—life-giving radiations
      of beauty, health,
           and spiritual prosperity
    shine out like rays of the sun.
Aspire to humility rather than power,
        prestige, and privilege; for
    grace and gentleness sustain the
        humble of heart.
As seed germinates in fertile soil,
    the Seed of Divine Thought
        will grow in soul-silence.
Ground yourself with deep roots
      in the Great Mystery.

Lumen Christi . . . Holy Wisdom.

Divine
Presence
is
revealed
in the
fullness
of
each
moment.

Do not let your life become rote, based
on issues of control
rather than spontaneous creativity.
Needed is a burning passion to attract
new expressions of gifts
given in the service of Love.
To develop and expand your heart's highest
aspiration, deepest awareness,
you may have to risk the unconventional.
Time spent in silence and solitude helps
awaken the soul, affording new
insights and guidance that point
the way to new life.
Procrastination renders will and action weak,
and often paralyzes intent.
Act now! Begin to shine with peace,
gladness, and harmony;
You will become a light for other pilgrims
who tread the spiritual path.

Lumen Christi . . . Holy Wisdom.

The
reality
of this
moment
is
Love
knowing
Itself.

A divided heart withers and wounds
the soul,
creating confusion and chaos
in body and mind.
Limited becomes the expression of joy,
love, and beauty: the birthright,
the truth of your Inner Being.
Constant attunement, holding to thoughts
that are life-giving,
brushes away references to past hurts
and fear of future calamities.
Awaken to the present moment!
Focus on loving aspirations:
your choice of thought creates
your daily life.
In trusting, chosen self-surrender allow
the Great Healer to lead the way
to wholehearted love
of self and others.

Lumen Christi . . . Holy Wisdom.

Listen!
Inner guidance
is yours
for
the asking.

Heed
the
call.

The time has come to awaken fully
from our long sleep,
to delight in creativity
and freedom
where the Source of all is evoked.
Commune in silence with the Divine Guest,
Beloved Companion of your soul.
Let not worldly powers or pursuits
lull us into inertia,
like worker drones in a beehive.
Let us recognize our extraordinary gifts
and potential
in the daily details. Let us
Pause often to listen for Divine Hints;
the time is Now!
The call to serve awaits our "yes."
Reverence life; honor the truth
of our interbeing with all of Creation.
Many in other realms travel with us.
Welcome them!

Lumen Christi . . . Holy Wisdom.

Illusion
and
ignorance
abound.

Embark
on a
continuous
search
for
the fullness
of
Wisdom.

Be aware of imbalances in every
            institution of learning!
When expressions of spiritual growth
            are ignored or squelched,
      rare are those who fly from
            the nest with wings to soar;
Creativity atrophies; work becomes
            drugery, like drugged sleep.
Lost is the spontaneity that reflects
                  wholeness and holiness.
Needed is salvation: a salvaging process
         to save all that is life-giving,
      to refine and redefine the dross
                  into truth.
Become a builder of the New Jerusalem,
         the Holy City that reflects
                  the Love and Light
            of your awakened consciousness.

      Lumen Christi . . . Holy Wisdom.

True communication:

Discovering
your
Self
in
communion
with
the
whole
community.

Delve into the heart of prayer!
      The deeper you dive,
      the more prayer will become a hunger;
A hunger that compels us to create regular
      nurturing pauses for silence
            and solitude.
Here we connect and commune with
      the authentic ground of our being,
            the Touchstone of Love.
Not for ourselves alone do we pray:
      for deep, contemplative prayer will surely
      lead to active, compassionate
            service.
We will become like laser beams of light,
      whose inner fire sets other hearts
            aflame:
      the inner, hidden work of Love.
Your prayer life makes a difference!
Become the prayer! Commune with All!

Lumen Christi . . . Holy Wisdom.

Ask Earth,

"What
can
I
do
for
you?"

Through the immensity of your Heart,
    refine our limited egos with
       the Fire of your Love.
To surrender willingly is to awaken to
          your Divine Presence,
    Ineffable Mystery: plentitude of Life.
As nature freely bestows her gifts,
    who among us pauses to acknowledge
    her life-giving support?
Awaken! Mother Earth is a living, vibrant,
       sacred being.
    Her wounds are scars upon our soul.
Help us, O Beloved, to build a world
       culture of the heart,
    where people from every nation form
    true community, where we all
Co-exist in harmony, peace, assurance,
       gratitude, and love.

Lumen Christi . . . Holy Wisdom.

May
peace and joy
ever radiate
from
your heart
as you
co-birth
in the
New Creation.

Watch for new revelations as the Veil
begins to fade away,
like clouds penetrated by rays
of brilliant sunshine.
Much will be revealed that has long
been hidden in mystery;
Prepare the way for Awakening!
Be not afraid to yield to the Unknown,
to become vulnerable and pliant:
the Beloved will lead you
to new life.
Trust the Holy Process, enjoy the Mystery!
Like Pentecost of old, wondrous changes
are even now emerging,
calling each of us to attune to the
music, to join in the Song.
Spend time in sacred space and listen.
Out of the Silence you may hear
your Invitation:
Come to the Dance!

Lumen Christi . . . Holy Wisdom.

Half the profits from *Lumen Christi . . . Holy Wisdom* will be divided between Friends of Silence, a non-profit endeavor to facilitate others in reverencing Silence, prayer, and contemplation, and to encourage the life-giving empowerment that derives from the Silence; and The Guild for Spiritual Guidance, a two-year apprentice program that seeks to develop a heightened awareness of "the many and diverse ways" God is present in and to the world.

For further information, write to:

FRIENDS OF SILENCE
129 SKUNK HOLLOW ROAD
JERICHO, VERMONT 05465